LIFTED

Dr. Gilbert,

We are so blessed that God uses you in so many special ways.

Dr. [illegible signature]

DR. SYLVIA CRUDUP & DR. JAMES BETHEA

LIFTED

a young person's guide to self-motivation & success

TATE PUBLISHING & *Enterprises*

Lifted

Published by Tate Publishing & Enterprises, LLC
127 E. Trade Center Terrace | Mustang, Oklahoma 73064 USA
1.888.361.9473 | www.tatepublishing.com

Tate Publishing is committed to excellence in the publishing industry. The company reflects the philosophy established by the founders, based on Psalm 68:11,
"The Lord gave the word and great was the company of those who published it."

Cover design by Kellie Southerland
Interior design by Lindsay B. Behrens

Published in the United States of America

ISBN: 978-1-61739-528-4
Self-Help / Personal Growth / Success
10.12.06

Acknowledgements

For Dr. Sylvia Crudup:
Some people have profoundly influenced my life. Others have contributed much to me either personally or professionally.

I want to thank my immediate family, including my son, Donza Ricardo Cole; my sister, Lena Marie Johnson; and my two nephews, Fred and Jermaine Johnson.

Some friends and colleagues who have helped and encouraged me in various ways include Dr. Will Reid, Dr. Jim Conner, Ms. Florence Jean Wright,

Bishop Arizona Hartsfield, Jacque Montgomery, Dr. Jane Finneran, Sam Lajoh, and Ruth Williams.

Finally, thanks to my long standing mentor, Dr. Dudley Flood, whose profound influence runs through all that I do and say in my professional life.

For Dr. Bethea:
Throughout the course of my life I have been positively impacted by many people. Of particular importance are my mother, Margaret Pate; my sister, Barbara Bethea; my best friend, Patrick Medley; and my mentor, Dr. James K. Gripper III. Thank you for helping to shape and mold me to become the person I am today.

I would also like to acknowledge my colleague, mentor, and friend, Dr. Sylvia Crudup, for seeing this vision come to fruition. Your perseverance and resilience are admirable.

Finally, to my wife, Martina and my sons, Alaye, Armon, and Aaris. You are *sina qua non* for my *rasion d'etre*.

Table of Contents

Just for You

> By virtue of being born to humanity, every human being has a right to the development and fulfillment of his [her] potentialities as a human being.
>
> —Ashley Montagu

Ashley Montagu's words hold true for everyone. No matter where you start in life, every human being has a right to succeed. We succeed by fulfilling our potential as human beings. We are born with equal rights and special talents. However, to use our special talents, we must be able to dream, set goals, and follow a plan of action to achieve our goals. This little book was written to show you how.

Sometimes we give up on our dreams because we think we do not have what we need. Some young people give up because they have few or no "significant others" to cheer them on. We wrote this little book to give you the support you need and help you pave a pathway to your dreams. We want you to succeed, even if you may not have the support of family, friends, or significant others. Ultimately, if you are to be all you can be, you must be self-motivated and really want to succeed.

We want you to reach your full potential and maintain motivation throughout life. As used in this book, self-motivation is doing what you have to do, with or without help, whether you want to or not.

Benjamin Elijah Mays, minister, educator, and civil rights activist, said, "It is not your environment, it is you——the quality of your mind, the integrity of your soul, and the determination of your will——that will decide your future and shape your life ..." It is truly up to you how successful you will be. According to philanthropist Andrew Carnegie, the difference between average people and truly successful people is not IQ or education but the degree of self-motivation they have. When you really want to, you will seek ways to turn dreams into goals and develop a plan to reach your goals.

To be all you can be, you need self-knowledge, realistic goals, a plan, key people to help, and self-motivation. Your passion and your desire will drive you. If you do not have passion and desire, you are more likely to be satisfied doing nothing of significance in life, and you will probably try, at all cost, to avoid criticism.

According to U.S. author Elbert Hubbard, "To avoid criticism: do nothing, say nothing, be nothing." We, your authors, want more for you. We want you to achieve what you want in life. *We expect you to succeed.*

This little book tells you how to find motivation from within and maintain self-motivation throughout life. We expect you to dream, set goals, and succeed. The following questions are keys in your quest for success:

- Do I Desire Success?
- Do I Need A Mentor?
- What Are My Dreams?

- How Do I Express Myself?
- How Will I Know My Self-Worth?
- What Natural Talents and Abilities Do I Have?
- What Is Self-Talk?

Do I Desire Success?

> Life takes on meaning when you become motivated, set goals, and charge after them in an unstoppable manner.
>
> —Les Brown

It is hard to know just how much passion and desire it takes to be successful. Winning and reaching goals seldom come easy, and many people give up the minute they become frustrated. Shawn Lim's story demonstrates how burning desire must become a must for you.

> Long ago, there is a King, and he wants to conquer an island. The King orders a General to handle this mission. The King only gives the General 100 soldiers. The enemy has 1,000 soldiers guarding that island. So how is this general going to win this war? They are outnumbered.
>
> What the General did was burn all the ships that carried his men to the island. Now, there is no way back, it is either kill or be killed. The General leaves his men no choice but to win the war. In the end, they did win the war.

The moral of the story is, if you want something so badly, you have to eliminate the option of retreat.

Be passionate about succeeding! Whatever you desire in life, you should want to succeed at it. Also, what you desire to achieve in life must dominate your thoughts. They must become your driving force daily. When you are passionate about succeeding, you take risks and open up to others about what you want to achieve. You reveal your dreams and aspirations and seek ways to achieve them every opportunity you get. You charge after your dreams and goals in a manner that motivational speaker Les Brown describes as "unstoppable."

To be successful in life, you will probably be criticized. Being criticized is something that happens to everyone. When you become passionate about what you want to do, you are not afraid of being criticized. You do not allow fear of criticism to hinder you or stop you from dreaming. Successful people use criticism as a motivator. The trick is to take advice that is helpful and remove the rest. If you listen to criticisms carefully, many times, you can find words of wisdom. Listen well, and remember to thank people for their comments. Somewhere in their comments is something you can use to your advantage. Don't spend time being defensive or justifying what you want to do, just listen and learn, even when people are critical and discouraging.

Sometimes negative comments or negative influences come from people you cannot easily get away from like friends, teachers, and even family members. However, take what you can use, and seek caring adults who can help you sort things out and move forward. Find the things you love and go after them. Whatever it is you really want in life, just go for it.

That's what we call "passion." Be passionate about what is important to you!

> I want you to be everything that's you, deep at the center of your being.
>
> —Confucius

Do I Need A Mentor?

> A hundred years from now it will not matter the sort of house I lived in, what my bank account was or the kind of car I drove, but the world may be different because I was important in the life of a child.
>
> —author unknown

There was a tropical island a few miles off the coast. One day all the birds assembled. They decided they needed to select a leader who could help them all get along as a group. How would they select? The parrot thought it should be the one with the brightest color.

The ostrich thought it should be the one with best plumage. The hummingbird suggested it be one who could fly backwards. The hawk suggested eyesight.

After much discussion, they agreed on a contest. The bird that could fly the highest could be selected as leader. They all gathered in a clearing with an unobstructed view. One by one, each bird took off and flew as high as he or she could. The hawk and falcon used their keen eyesight to determine how high each bird flew. At the very end it was the eagle's turn. He flew up and up and up, higher than any other bird had flown. The crowd chirped and squawked and crowed and quacked and honked to applaud the eagle.

"Wait," cried the falcon. "There is something higher than the eagle." The hawks and falcons and other birds zeroed in on this tiny speck in the sky. Finally, the falcon cried, "It's a sparrow. It's a sparrow!"

When both the eagle and sparrow landed, the crowd of birds rushed over to their new leader, the sparrow. They asked, "How did you do it? You were the best."

The sparrow looked at the eagle and said, "I had help. When the eagle took off, I was sitting on his back. When he was exhausted and could fly no higher, I took off from his back and flew even higher than the eagle."

The birds cheered the sparrow and cheered the eagle. A discussion was held and the group decided their new leader should be the eagle. He showed what true leadership was when he used his strength and skills to help another succeed.

This story illustrates the type of leadership mentors generally have. They use their leadership, skills, and abilities to help others reach their goals. Believe it or not, everyone needs a mentor.

You need people and mentors. Right now, you may not know just how important caring adults and mentors are in turning your dreams into goals. It is easier to reach goals when you have the support of caring adults. Most adults are happy to help young people get where they are going in life. Sometimes support comes from parents, relatives, friends, and role models. When you do not have these supportive people in your life, you definitely need a mentor, *and* you really need self-motivation.

Without help and support, it is easy to slip off course. You become unfocused, confused, and lose sight of your dreams and true purpose in life. A mentor can help you stay focused and make sure you reach your goals. Most coaches have mentors, and so should you. Use your mentor well since mentoring is not a lifetime relationship. A mentor, usually someone a little older than you, guides you and coaches you along the way until you no longer need his or her help.

Is there someone in your life right now who can help you?

Do you know an adult right now who you could ask to be your mentor?

Even if you have a supportive family, it is still a good idea to have a mentor. Some young people do not have supportive families and have to go it alone. If you are one who must go it alone without supportive family members, *you really need a mentor!*

If you have trouble knowing which adults you can count on, watch what they do. Look especially at adults who care about you and are understanding. When identifying caring adults, try to talk to other young people they have helped. Identify qualities these adults possess that you like. Ask other people what they think of this person and study him or her carefully. Talk to them about their successes, and then ask them to mentor you.

This process will help steer you to adults who can be role models and mentors. Again, you must be able to recognize a mentor and be willing to ask that person if he or she will mentor you. Some people will volunteer to be your mentor, but others will need to be asked. If you truly want to succeed, you must know you are worthy of having a mentor. Just ask any successful adult if they had a mentor at some point in their lives, and over half of them will probably say "yes." Well-intending adults love to mentor young people who want to do something positive in life.

In looking for a mentor, you want a person who can help you get off to a good start in life. Good mentors see mentoring as one of the most important contributions they can make in life. Remember, however, some people do not see themselves as mentors. Therefore, people have a right to say "no." Do not take this personally, should this happen. You would not want a person to mentor you when mentoring is not their calling.

Hopefully, you will ask adults for help who are successful at their own career endeavors. Usually adults interview young people, but in this case, you are interviewing them. You are the one choosing a mentor, not the other way around.

Here are some things a good mentor can do for you. A good mentor can help you when your self-esteem is low. A good mentor can help you find the right contacts for jobs before you leave high school or assist you in identifying good schools for further study.

Your mentor may be instrumental in getting part-time work or an internship before you graduate from high school. Internships are mostly unpaid work opportunities, but you gain valuable experience to be included on your resume or in your portfolio. Your mentor may also help you contact employers for job shadowing opportunities. In job shadowing, you are allowed to observe a person in a position of interest at the work place. You watch them work to decide whether this is the type of work you see yourself doing in the future. Your mentor can help you achieve your dreams and help you set realistic goals or put you in touch with someone who can.

Your school counselor and teachers can be helpful in identifying these opportunities for you too.

All these experiences, paid or unpaid, should be part of your resume or portfolio. In a resume, you outline your education, work experiences, and interests to present to potential employers. Some prospective employers will ask you for a resume or simply accept a completed job application. A portfolio is a collection of samples of your work that you include in a notebook or binder. You would also include photographs of awards, copies of certificates, letters of appreciation, and recommendations from people like community leaders or employers. Your mentor can help you put all this information in the format necessary for success or help identify someone to assist you. People help us achieve our dreams and goals. Start now paying close attention to adults who can help you get where you need to go in life. Be the best communicator you can be and start making good impressions.

Seeking caring adults to serve as mentors is a process. Be careful. Ask questions about adults before you ask them to lead you. You don't want to be led astray. There are some adults who prey on young people who have little or no parental support. Sometimes it is not easy to identify pedophiles, drug dealers, and professional criminals. These people operate in the real world too and should be avoided. Be aware of this and be careful!

Before selecting a mentor, here are key questions to ask.

1. Who have you seen performing in the role of a mentor?
2. If you know someone who could be a potential mentor, have they given you good advice in the past?
3. How do you know these potential mentors are successfully engaged in some legal line of work?
4. How do you know about these potential mentors' accomplishments?

List the names of adults who you think would make good mentors.

____

____

____

To reach goals, you will have to work hard. You may also make mistakes along the way. However, having caring adults to confide in will keep you going. To stay motivated, it helps to have significant others to cheer you on.

1. Are you ready to ask any potential mentors you just listed to be your mentor? If not, what will it take to get you ready?

____

____

2. If you need assistance, who can help you get ready to ask one of these individuals to be your mentor?

____

> Instruction does much, but encouragement does everything.
>
> —Johann Wolfgang von Goethe

What Are My Dreams?

Climb high, climb far, your goal the sky, your aim the stars.

—Anonymous

Hope is a waking dream.

—Aristotle

Orville and Wilbur Wright were two brothers with one dream—one very big dream—to invent the airplane!

Although they could envision it, people had a tough time accepting the notion of people flying through the air. In fact, their father, Bishop Milton Wright, said "Flight [is] reserved for the birds and the angels."

The desire to invent was directly connected to the brothers' mother, a college graduate who was always "fixing or making things." It was she who taught them to make their very own snow sleds.

Orville and Wilbur decided to test their ideas on flying machines using their experiences with a toy helicopter, kites, bicycles, and a printing machine. Starting with gliders, Orville and Wilbur tested over 200 different wings before building one with a motor.

When the brothers got tired of people inquiring about their planes, they said simply, "The plane stays up because it doesn't have time to fall."

After failed attempts and crashing, Orville and Wilbur continued working, never giving up on their dream. Realizing it was time, on December 17, 1903, they tried another flight at Kitty Hawk, North Carolina. They made history! Orville flew twelve seconds successfully, and life for them was changed forever.

You must dream big and set goals. If you are one who says you have no goals, please stop saying this now. Everyone has dreams and goals. Goal setting is simply writing down what you want to do in life and writing objectives (steps to take to achieve the goal). To accomplish your goals, you must dream. You must dream and dream big. Then you pursue your dreams by writing them as goals. Goals are dreams put to action.

Dreaming is easy, but it takes work to turn dreams into reality.

Turning dreams into goals is a step-by-step process. It is a plan. For example, if the goal is to make better grades, you have to set objectives in order to reach the goal. Objectives are those things you commit to in order to achieve the goal. With timetables established for each objective, you have a concrete way of knowing when you have accomplished each objective to reach your goal.

If the goal is to improve your grades, one objective may be to work with a tutor once a week. A second objective may be to do homework or study for two hours each day after school. A third objective may be to turn in *all* homework on time.

The steps we take to reach our goals are our objectives. Objectives are measurable. Objectives are the keys to reaching goals. They answer the question, "How will I reach my goals?"

Objectives give you timelines so you can see when you have accomplished each step. When objectives are well written with timelines, you can check yourself daily or weekly and ask, "Did I do what I said I would do in my objectives?" Your answer will always be a definite yes or no when objectives are written with specific times to get things done.

There are certain things you must do before getting something as simple as a driver's license. List the objectives (steps) you must take to become a licensed driver (your goal).

____

____

____

____

In achieving goals, you always write out objectives so you can see how to reach your goals. In the exercise you just completed, your goal was to become a licensed driver. The objectives were the things you had to do to get your license. This is what you have to do with all goals. All goals and objectives should be written down and should have deadlines.

This is a process all people of greatness take to achieve their goals. First, they talk to enough people to get some idea about who they are and what their capabilities are. Most caring adults are glad to help you find your way. Remember, goals must be realistic to maintain the self-motivation needed to achieve them. Caring adults can help you set realistic goals——those you can actually achieve.

Secondly, people who achieve their goals identify people who are doing what they may want to do. Many of these people will have completed high school and may have obtained education beyond high school. They put activities in place to reach their goals. Talking with people about how they achieved the results they wanted can be a valuable experience. Identify some people today and ask them to share their insights and secrets for succeeding.

Who do you want to be when you grow up, or who do you want to be like? Who is doing something similar to what you would like to do someday? Write your answers in the spaces provided.

____

____

____

Successful people had to take these steps to realize their dreams. No one did this for them. You too must do this. Never worry that a goal is too big. Big goals force you to dream big, stretch yourself, and push forward in the midst of adversity. Big goals give the strength, willpower, and determination to handle life's difficulties. Never worry about how many goals you have either. You can always change them. *Nothing, absolutely nothing,* is set in stone. Just set some goals and never lose sight of them. Professional race car driver Mario Andretti reminds us that, "Circumstances may cause interruptions and delays, but never lose sight of your goal." If you feel strongly enough about your goals, you will find ways to achieve them.

By the way, finishing high school should be a goal for everyone. Some objectives for this goal would be things such as attending classes daily, studying daily, doing all homework, and passing exams.

> There are some people who live in a dream world, and there are some who face reality; and then there are those who turn one into the other.
>
> —Douglas Everett

> Every day do something that will inch you closer to a better tomorrow.
>
> —Doug Firebaugh

Write one goal that is important to you. List the objectives (steps) you must complete to reach the goal.

Goal with deadline date:

____

____

Objectives with timelines:

How Do I Express Myself?

> When you exercise your freedom to express yourself at the lowest level, you ultimately condemn yourself to live at that level.
>
> —Zig Ziglar

Communication can sometimes be hard as seen in D. Anderson's Dixie Quack. Dixie lives in a barnyard with five brothers and sisters. Dixie has feathers. She has webbed feet. She has a beak. Dixie is like any other duck except for one thing. Dixie doesn't like to quack. She's growing up and her voice wants to quack, but she wants to cheep. The result is a very funny: *chee-WACK.*

"You're growing up and must learn to quack," says Dixie's mother.

Ruffling her downy feathers she asks, "Why?"

"It's how we talk, to show if we're happy or in trouble, to warn of danger and mommy ducks quack so their ducklings can follow her," she said. But Dixie wanted to do something different.

She spent all day exploring the bardyard and imitating other animals. She barked, meowed, mooed, and snorted. She even crowed like Red the Rooster, but that hurt her throat, so she quit. Dixie liked meowing best. She told mother duck from now on she would meow and not quack.

"Okay, if that is what you want," mother duck said. "Now go to sleep. Tomorrow we're leaving the barnyard and going to the pond." Dixie slept that night, her beak tucked under her wings, and dreamed of animals and the sounds they make.

The next morning Dixie, her mother, and her five siblings all waddled to the pond. It was the first time any of the ducklings had been out of the barnyard and were very excited!

Dixie's siblings chirped and quacked to each other, and just as she promised, Dixie meowed. But her brothers and sisters didn't meow to her. In fact, none of them seemed to understand her! Dixie was starting to feel left out. As they swam Dixie looked around the wide-open pond in amazement. It was much bigger than their pond in the barnyard.

Dixie spied a little grasshopper on a leaf that looked very tasty, but it jumped away. She swam to the next leaf, but it jumped again. Dixie kept chasing it until it jumped on the grass and disappeared.

Dixie swam to catch up with her family. They were nowhere to be found. Dixie realized she was lost! Dixie was scared! Then she remembered her mother said to call out if she got lost. Dixie meowed as loud as she could. No one answered. Dixie tried every animal sound she knew: barking, mooing, snorting, and even the rooster's crow. No one answered. Dixie tucked her head under her wing and cried. Then, she heard someone quack. It was her mother!

Dixie opened up her beak to answer and what came out was not a moo, not a meow or a snort or a bark. It was definitely not a rooster's crow. Dixie shouted, "*Quack!*" Her family came swimming up, very glad to see her. As Dixie's mother put a soft wing around her she said, "Aren't you glad you can quack?" Dixie answered her with a very proud "Quack!"

You must communicate well. The two main ways you communicate are through what you say and how you look. People make judgments about you based on what you say and how you look, whether you like it or not. People size you up quickly, so you must make a positive impression on people, especially those you need to ask for help.

How do you speak when you meet people of influence? Your authors know from experience after experience that, "Hi, I am (name) and would love to talk with you about ..." is a great starter for any conversation. No one can criticize this approach.

How do you generally dress? Are you well groomed? The impression you make on people may impact your life immediately or it may impact your life later. At any rate, if you know showing stomach skin, exposing cleavage, or wearing baggy pants well below your waist will not make a favorable impression, then don't do it.

Most adults who can help you do not appreciate your presenting yourself in ways other than traditional dress. This is because if they take you under their wing, or mentor you in any way, you represent them, and they want to be represented with dignity and respect. When you insist on departing too much from traditional dress codes, it makes people wonder, "Is he or she really serious about what they say they want to do?"

When you enter a work setting or learning environment using foul language, wearing baggy, sagging pants, or showing cleavage and stomach, this makes people question your desire to fit in. You will simply be left wondering why you didn't get a second meeting or why you didn't get the job or whatever you were seeking.

Decide what you want, and be willing to adjust your way of doing things to get the things in life that are important to you. Learn to speak the King's English and stop cursing if you have inadvertently taken on this habit.

Remember, your first impression will never be forgotten. And remember, Dixie had to follow the norm to communicate effectively.

Watch your thoughts. They become words. Watch your words. They become actions. Watch your actions. They become habits. Watch your habits. They become character. Watch your character. It becomes your destiny.

—author unknown

How Will I Know My Self-Worth?

> My sense of my own importance to myself is tremendous. I am all I have to work with, to suffer and to enjoy. It is not the eyes of others that I am wary of, but my own.
>
> —Noel Coward

Have you ever read Jael Ravalyn's *A Dragon Makes A Friend & Panda Gets A Campfire?* In this story, a lonely dragon wants a friend and tries to make friends with people. But every time he meets people they end up getting scared because when he sneezes, fire comes out of his nose!

Poor Dragon! He decided he should just go. Dragon flew off into the jungle to get far away from others. In the distance, he saw a funny black and white bush by a pile of wood. Dragon decided he would go sit by that bush since it had seemed lonely around all the green plants, and Dragon knew what it was like to be lonely. But the bush was not a bush at all. It was a fluffy great panda!

Dragon got worried because he needed to sneeze and thought the Panda would get scared. But it was too late. *Uh-uh-choooooo!* Dragon couldn't stop it; he sneezed!

Panda got up and looked at Dragon. "Did you do that?" Panda asked.

"Yes, I did," said Dragon sadly hanging his head.

"Thank you!" Panda said happily. "You made a fire with my sticks! I tried and tried so hard and just could not get the fire to start. Come on and sit by me and we can warm up on this cool night by the fire. Want some bamboo?"

Dragon was so excited he had finally made a friend who was not scared of him for sneezing! Panda helped Dragon see his sneezes might come in handy.

You must know yourself, love yourself, and know your self-worth. Do you interact with people who care about you and tell you how valuable you are as a person? To motivate yourself and aspire for greatness, you must have a clear picture about your worth. This is tied directly to your ability to feel good about yourself and love yourself. Loving yourself is about appreciating yourself and knowing how valuable you are. When you know how valuable you are, you do things that bring you closer to the things you want in life.

Do you know who values you and why they value you? To love yourself is not to be selfish but to think of yourself in terms of your worth, your value, and the special gifts you possess. It's really about appreciating who you are. To appreciate yourself, you must have high feelings of self-worth and lots of self-confidence.

How does one gain this kind of worth and self-confidence? You have to talk to people. You have to talk to enough people who know you well to find out how people perceive you. Get them to tell you what your strong points are. Ask them to point out particular strengths you possess. Then weigh these against how you perceive yourself. Is the way you perceive yourself close to the way others perceive you?

Some questions you can ask yourself to assess your value are these. Do you have skills that other people use? Are you good at things that employers want in employees? Are you especially helpful at home? Have you helped someone lately? If your answer is yes, then you have good reasons to feel good about yourself. If your answer is no, then you need to get busy talking to as many people as possible to identify some ways to increase your self-worth. Using your strong points and strengths in meaningful ways to help others is one way you can enhance your worth and value as a person.

Knowing who you are means you know your strengths and true potential. This helps you determine where you are headed in life. You can set realistic goals and take steps to reach your goals when you know your purpose and potential. Goals are generally tied to your purpose in life, and everyone has a purpose. Dr. Gary Moore, professor at North Carolina

State University at Raleigh, always said, "A ship with no port of destination knows no favorable wind." Think about that! This is true. One of the quickest ways to identify your true potential is by talking with enough caring adults who know you well. These caring adults can give you clues to who you are and where you are headed.

The quicker you know who you are, the quicker you can realize your dreams. Seeing yourself actually doing what you want to do is called visualization. Do you have a vision of your future? If yes, visualize where you want to go and who you want to be. Take a moment now to actually see yourself reaching your goal. How does it feel? Are you satisfied? Do you actually see yourself where you want to be? Visualization is a giant step beyond just dreaming. If you can envision it, you can achieve it!

Are you happy about what you have achieved so far in school, at home, and in your community? Most people dream of who they want to be but have no real plan to get where they are going. You can become the person you want to be, but you must be self-motivated and have a plan. It is hard to motivate yourself if you are not comfortable with whom you are. When you look in the mirror, are you comfortable in the skin you are in? Can you see all the good things about you?

Look in the mirror each day and say, "I am lovable and capable." Each day is a new day, regardless of what happened yesterday. We all wake up each morning with our invisible IALAC sign, which means *I am lovable and capable.* Each day it gets ripped by peoples' put-downs or things you don't get right. However, each day you get to start over again because you are still lovable and capable, regardless of what happened yesterday. You just have to remember you have the right to become all you can be.

When you truly feel good about yourself, you are more careful about the friends you choose. Are your friends looking for opportunities to succeed or constantly coming up with excuses why they are not? It is almost impossible to stay focused and motivated to achieve your goals in the midst of people who are pessimistic and not supportive of you. Do your friends have goals they want to achieve too? All possibilities of what you can do slip away quickly if you are surrounded by friends who are doing little to help themselves. When you are surrounded by negative, pessimistic people, all creativity and all desire quickly disappear. Just as enthusiasm, motivation, and inspiration are contagious, so too are negativity and pessimism.

Do your friends participate in high-risk activities? Engaging in high-risk activities like drug use, sex, and alcohol can kill your dreams. These activities should be avoided at all cost. Nobody plans to become addicted to drugs. Nobody plans to have a baby before they are ready. Nobody plans to get drunk and crash a car, but it happens. Try to avoid these temptations, especially at this stage in your life. Sometimes these activities will come to you by way of your friends. Some people work hard at getting others to engage in high-risk and illegal activities. These people do not believe they can realize their dreams and, therefore, work hard to interrupt the process for others. That's why you must choose your friends wisely! When you can, stay away from people who discourage you or try to engage you in high-risk activities. Learn to say "no" without insulting or putting people down. Try to surround yourself with friendly, supportive people and people who are achievers. Choose friends who have goals like you and desire good things in life. There is power when like-minded individuals work together to achieve goals! You don't get to pick your family or childhood experiences, but you do get to choose your friends and your direction in life.

How you treat yourself is just as important as who you choose as friends. Do you exercise, eat well, and get plenty of rest? I bet you are saying to yourself, "What does this have to do with self-motivation and success?" This attention to the physical self has a lot to do with your mental attitude. It takes willpower and discipline to take good care of yourself, just like it takes willpower and discipline to achieve goals. They are connected.

Doing things like staying active physically, eating well, and getting proper rest and sleep challenge you both physically and mentally. Staying motivated to get things done also challenges you mentally and physically. These challenges help you stay motivated.

Just being motivated to get things done takes sheer willpower. Doing things that take lots of self-discipline may seem hard at first. This is why you must have ways of reenergizing and rejuvenating yourself.

What you are striving for is a healthy body and a healthy mind. It's up to you to have a positive or negative attitude about things. You must continuously think positive thoughts and see yourself winning rather than failing. Others are watching you. If you are positive and take good care of yourself, they may be inspired to do likewise.

Don't forget to physically exercise daily. Frequent workouts help to reduce stress and cut down on anxiety or feelings of frustration. Whenever you feel overwhelmed, just do some deep breathing (taking in air through your nose and exhaling through your mouth). If you have more time, take a quick jog, a spin on your bike, do a fun thing, laugh, or whatever will rejuvenate you quickly.

Your attitude will make or break you. What you give and get from life is determined ultimately by how you see yourself and how self-motivated you are. You are in charge of how well you take care of yourself. Taking charge of your attitude and actions is a giant step in the right direction.

Associate yourself with men [women] of good quality if you esteem your own reputation; for 'tis better to be alone than in bad company.

—George Washington

Patience, persistence, and perspiration make an unbeatable combination for success.

—Napoleon Hill

What Natural Talents and Abilities Do I Have?

> The Creator has not given you a longing to do that which you have no ability to do.
>
> —Orison Swett Marden

To keep going when people say you can't is a valuable skill. Henry Ford had this skill. He knew himself well. He knew his abilities and capitalized on his strengths. He also knew failure, but failure for him did not mean quit. For him it meant starting again more intelligently.

Ford invented what was called the horseless carriage when people thought he couldn't. His first company failed, but he did not give up. He was always willing to take risks and try new things.

After Ford's Model T, many innovations followed including one of the most popular cars ever—the Mustang. But was Henry Ford an overnight success? Not by a long shot. Failure came upon him many times before success, but Ford knew failure was no indication that he should give up. To be a winner you must see failure as Ford did—an opportunity to start over more intelligently.

You must know your natural talents, strengths, and abilities. Successful people find their strengths and capitalize on them. They concentrate on their strengths, not their weaknesses. They don't try to improve on weaknesses. Successful people understand it would be too hard and take too long to attempt to turn weaknesses into strengths. Therefore, they take their strengths and do as pro basketball coach Red Auerbach says, "Just do what you do best."

You have more potential and many more strengths than you think you have. Are you able to identify your strengths? Knowing your strengths gives you a better idea of where you are headed. Your strengths will give you a *realistic view of what you can accomplish.* Focus on your strengths, and build your goals around them.

Most people never use all their talents and abilities. Research findings indicate that average people use only between 5 to 10 percent of their potential. This means most people have untapped resources. They have gifts, talents, and ability *they never use.* Don't let this happen to you. Start now using all your talent, ability, strengths, and resources. Be the best you can be, and always do the best you can in whatever you undertake. Stop believing people who put you down, and start believing in yourself.

You develop natural talents and abilities by doing things. You start by focusing on things you do well and setting more goals. Make it a habit to do more than is expected of you. Do more homework than is assigned by your teacher. There is always a need to read, even if there is no homework. Do more chores at home than you are asked to do. Do what you do best over and over again, and do them even better. This is how you make good use of natural talents and build skills.

This is the process most successful people take to identify their natural talents and strengths. They talk to enough people to discover who they really are. Then they use this information to focus and improve their skills.

In life, you have both successes and failures but many more successes than failures. Push yourself to take risks so you can have both successes and failures. Remember Henry Ford's words, "Failure is the chance to begin again more intelligently." Success comes with practice from doing things. You have to take on some tasks if you are going to learn anything. The more you take on, the better you know what you can really do. Making mistakes is an important part of learning! Mistakes should not undermine your self-confidence. If you try to avoid mistakes, you will cease to learn. Successful people make mistakes too, but go on with succeeding.

The greatest speakers have to deliver speech after speech after speech before they are comfortable delivering what becomes some of the greatest speeches of all time.

Pro athletes spend hours and hours practicing their sport day after day after day. They don't become great overnight. While in school, these outstanding athletes still have to study and make good grades to remain active in their chosen sports.

The best hair designers perform their art over and over before they become good at hair design.

Great dancers spend hours daily not only practicing in their field but also following certain regimes to keep their bodies in tip-top shape in order to dance.

Teachers have to become experts in their subject area before being certified to teach.

Auto mechanics have to repair numerous cars before becoming expert mechanics.

Remember, you have many more strengths than weaknesses. You are responsible for developing your natural talents, your gifts, and ability.

There is no reason why you should suffer from lack of achievements. Some people excel in sports, others in academics, and some excel in art. Some excel because of their skills in areas like human relations. Some people know early what they are good at, and others learn later. Decide each day to do what you do best. Focus on these things, and do not lose sight of the course you must take.

You can do anything you set your mind to do. Your dreams, combined with your strengths, will enable you to motivate yourself. Everyone has ability, talents, and strengths, *and* everyone should have dreams.

When you have discipline and control over your life, you motivate yourself to do more. You can look in the mirror and tell yourself how special and strong you are. You also know you have something special to offer your home, community, and society.

Look at the following sentences. Refer to them often.

> I am responsible for developing my natural talents and abilities.
> I am aware of my strengths, special gifts, talents, and resources.
> I am able to set goals.
> Even if alone, I can establish objectives to achieve my goals.
> I can reach my goals.

Remember, don't let people tell you that you don't have special skills, talents, and gifts. Don't listen to those who tell you what you can't do with your talent, skills, and God-given gifts. Believe in yourself! Get busy now turning dreams into reality, and use all your potential to stay motivated.

> My business is not to remake myself, but to make the absolute best of what God made.
>
> —Robert Browning

> There is no meaning to life except the meaning man [woman] gives his [her] life by the unfolding of his [her] powers.
>
> —Eric Fromm

List ten of your strengths.

1.
2.
3.
4.
5.
6.
7.
8.
9.
10.

Ask a supportive adult who knows you well to list five of your strengths.

1.
2.
3.
4.
5.

How similar are the two lists? Do certain strengths appear on both lists?

What Is Self-Talk?

> The greatest revolution of our generation is the discovery that human beings, by changing the inner attitudes of their minds can change the outer aspects of their lives.
>
> —William James

One of the most famous books first printed in 1939 is *The Little Engine That Could.* The theme of the book is "I think I can."

I worked with a student in a Virginia Beach alternative high school who had experienced one failure after another and just did not have the will to continue trying. Finally, I asked him to read *The Little Engine That Could.*

You may recall the little engine took a heavy train over a hill that two other larger and stronger engines declined. The thing which ultimately helped the little engine over the hill was its own voice saying, "I think I can."

As this student jumped hurdle after hurdle, the worst being to retake and pass a test required for graduation, he feared he would not pass. As we studied for the exam, when fear got the best of him, I would remind him of the little engine.

Later, after passing the test he thanked me for what I considered a small act of kindness—to remind him of the little engine. I knew he could pass that test, but he had to change his self-talk and send a success message to himself just like the little engine.

You must control your thoughts and self-talk. Self-talk is one of the most powerful motivators there is in life. What you say to yourself about yourself is what we call "self-talk." The direction your life takes depends heavily on your self-talk. The messages you send your subconscious mind shape what you do throughout life. Self-talk is powerful!

If you think positively about yourself, it is easier for others to encourage you, support you, and help you stay motivated. If you fill your subconscious mind with negative thoughts, you limit yourself. Negative thoughts get in the way of setting positive goals. The more positive thoughts you can send yourself, the better off you are because more people will want to help you. People love to be around people who think positive thoughts.

Now that you have a better handle on your strengths and natural talents, try to identify yourself more positively and modify your self-talk. If you have been sending yourself negative thoughts of despair and defeat, you can change this. You can change the messages you send yourself. You can send positive messages to replace the negative ones.

Self-talk is tied very closely to what you believe you can become in life. Remember, it does not matter where you come from; what matters is where you are going. No matter what the circumstances, you still choose your course in life.

You can choose to fill your mind with what is positive about you rather than what is negative. If you choose to fill your mind with what is positive about you, this positive thinking changes your self-perception. Only you can do this, however. You do this by watching what you say about yourself to yourself. You also remove other peoples' negative comments from your mind. Other peoples' negative attitudes can wear you down and destroy your chances for success!

Everyone receives negative messages sooner or later. However, you don't need to say negative, degrading things about yourself. Aren't enough people just waiting to do that for you? So stop saying things like, "That teacher doesn't like me. Nobody cares about me. I can't get anything right. I'm dumb." Be aware of what you think and say. You are in control of your self-talk.

If someone says you are dumb, stupid, too big, too small, or gives you other negative messages, this tends to lower your feelings of self-worth. It causes low self-esteem. If you do not know many positive things about yourself, ask a caring adult to help you identify some.

It is hard to set positive goals with your mind dominated by negative thoughts. Talk to people who can help you plan positive things for your future. Additionally, every time you catch yourself thinking negative thoughts, tell yourself you are better than that. Send a positive thought to replace the negative one. Keep doing this until it becomes a habit.

Just as we learn to send negative messages to our subconscious mind, we can learn to send positive messages. Each time you catch yourself thinking a negative thought, tell yourself again you are better than that. If you make a habit of thinking positive thoughts, eventually, positive thoughts will dominate your mind. These positive thoughts will help build you up when others put you down.

Consider this. If you think you can't pass your test, it's likely you won't. If you think no one will read your poem, most likely, it won't be written. If you think you will be turned down, you probably won't ask. If you think you bring nothing to a job, you probably won't give it your best. You clearly get out of life what you think you can. Always try to pass good thoughts to your subconscious mind, and good things will often be the result.

In order to do anything of significance in life, you must be guided by good thoughts. Use your mind as your personal computer. You're familiar with the phrase "garbage in, garbage out." If you allow your mind to hold on to negative messages, you will doubt yourself, hold yourself back, and never use your true potential. Garbage is all you will have, and this will not motivate you. *Don't let this happen!* You can make it a habit to send your mind messages of success or messages of defeat. The choice is yours. Choose to send happy messages and messages of success, not failure.

Additionally, let's agree to stop beating up on yourself and start rewarding yourself with lots of positive self-talk. Don't be too hard on yourself when things don't go well. We are all disappointed in ourselves at times, but this is no reason to devalue yourself and label yourself unworthy, bad, or a loser. You have to recognize that you are a valuable person, regardless of what happens to you.

Here is another, and perhaps the most important, reason to fill your mind with positive thoughts. If you think positively about yourself, no difficulty is too tough for you to overcome, no test too hard, no peer pressure too powerful, nor will you stray far from your chosen path. Remember to remind yourself daily of affirmations to help you. Remind yourself that you are lovable, capable, and worthy of all good things in life.

Don't let anyone tell you that you should not have dreams and that you cannot reach your goals. You can be anything you want to be, but you must believe you can and plan for success. As we stated earlier, what you believe about yourself shapes your actions and the type of goals you set. Take some time to read about self-fulfilling prophecy. You have the potential to be what you want to be. If you do not, it's because you tell yourself you can't.

Positive thinking makes you more confident and happy about your future. Your mental strength comes from within. Therefore, you must control your own mind. It is okay to listen to others, but make decisions that are good for you. Your mind belongs to you. What you tell yourself you can do is basically what you will do. To be self-motivated, you must know deep down inside that you are special, gifted, and highly valued. You are born with this, and no one can take this away from you, unless you let them.

Remember, you can control much of what happens in your life!

> Whether you think you can or whether you think you can't, you're right!
>
> —Henry Ford

Final Words

> People often say that motivation doesn't last. Well, neither does bathing——that's why we recommend it daily.
>
> —Zig Ziglar

You are on a journey through life. You will make this trip whether you want to or not. Since you are on a journey, why not be the best you can be? Why not do something with your life to positively influence someone else? You are capable of being a major influence in the lives of others, no matter how young or inexperienced you are. Use your gifts and talents well.

All your talents, gifts, courage, and inner strength can work well for you. Your challenge is finding your way *and* making your mark. You are obligated to make your mark because *you were born with a purpose.* Even though life "throws you a curve" now and then, *you still have a good purpose in life.* Look from within, and that purpose will be revealed to you.

People who can motivate themselves tend to be winners. Self-motivated people experience failures, but they don't give up. A person who has never failed at something is generally a person who has not done much in life.

To succeed, you must motivate yourself daily. Life is made of many starts. We start, we stop, but we never quit. Life is also made of peaks and valleys, similar to a roller-coaster ride, but we don't quit. We may lose momentum, but we find hope and go on. This is how it's done. Keep making one step at a time, and never give up.

When you know your purpose in life, you never quit! You never give up. You persevere. Despite opposition, you continue. Despite what looks like failure, you still carry out the steps necessary to reach your goals. No matter how self-motivated you are, there will be some opposition along the way. You are expected to carry on despite opposition and setbacks. The reason you have to keep on going, despite the odds, is because *we expect you to.* When you are about to quit, think of people like Jake Simmons, Madame C. J. Walker, Henry Ford, Thomas Edison, Berry Gordy Jr., the Wright Brothers, Thomas Burrell, and your authors.

You have to decide the person you want to be and work at becoming that person daily. The key is that you recognize you are on equal footing with everyone else. Regardless of your start in life, you are of equal worth.

It is because of setbacks and disappointments that we doubt our true worth and value. Many people who have achieved great success in life have also dealt with feelings of low self-confidence and worth at some points. The difference is high achievers accept these feelings as valid, but not as reasons to give up on themselves. They still believe in themselves. They believe they can make their dreams come true and keep on going.

It takes lots of positive thinking and work to overcome things that interfere with your ability to love yourself and realize your true potential. You are among the best. You are capable, worthy, and strong. Behave that way. When you behave that way, you can motivate yourself to be the best you can be.

No matter what you have not done, let the words of Ashley Montagu be your guiding force in everything you attempt. "By virtue of being born to humanity, every human being has a right to the development and fulfillment of his [her] potentialities as a human being." Start now doing things to take you where you want to be in life. Do something everyday that takes you one step closer to some positive goal.

You may feel, at times, that you are literally on top of the world and, at other times, way down in the valley. Peaks and valleys do not make us powerless. They make us strong. They make us optimistic. They make us know that behind every storm cloud there is a silver lining. We wrote this little book to help you see how important it is to be self-motivated and know your potential. God put you here for a good purpose.

The essence of this little book is to help you see that where you go in life depends largely on your ability to motivate yourself. Remember, you can't make your dreams come true if you cannot visualize yourself reaching your goals. Remember also, a quitter never wins——and a winner never quits. You may become discouraged at times. This is expected, but do not quit. If you find yourself wanting to give up, remember your authors and remember the words of the poem, "Don't Quit." Refer to this poem often, and memorize it. Good luck!

> Inspiration comes from watching others. Motivation comes from within.
>
> —author unknown

Don't Quit

When things go wrong, as they sometimes will,
When the road you're trudging seems all up hill,
When the funds are low and the debts are high,
And you want to smile, but you have to sigh,
When care is pressing you down a bit,
Rest, if you must——but don't you quit.
Life is queer with its twists and turns,
As every one of us sometimes learns,
And many a failure turns about

When he might have won had he stuck it out;
Don't give up, though the pace seems slow——
You might succeed with another blow.
Often the goal is nearer than
It seems to a faint and faltering man,
Often the struggler has given up
When he might have captured the victor's cup.
And he learned too late, when the night slipped down,
How close he was to the golden crown.
Success is failure turned inside out——
The silver tint of the clouds of doubt——
And you never can tell how close you are,
It may be near when it seems afar;
So stick to the fight when you're hardest hit——
It's when things seem worst that you mustn't quit.

—author unknown

The most important goal for me right now is to:

____

____

Did you include a deadline for your goal?

List objectives (steps) for achieving your goal with timelines.

Do you have another goal that is important to you? If so, write it here, and include objectives as before.